TIME for KiDS

GOOD DOGS!

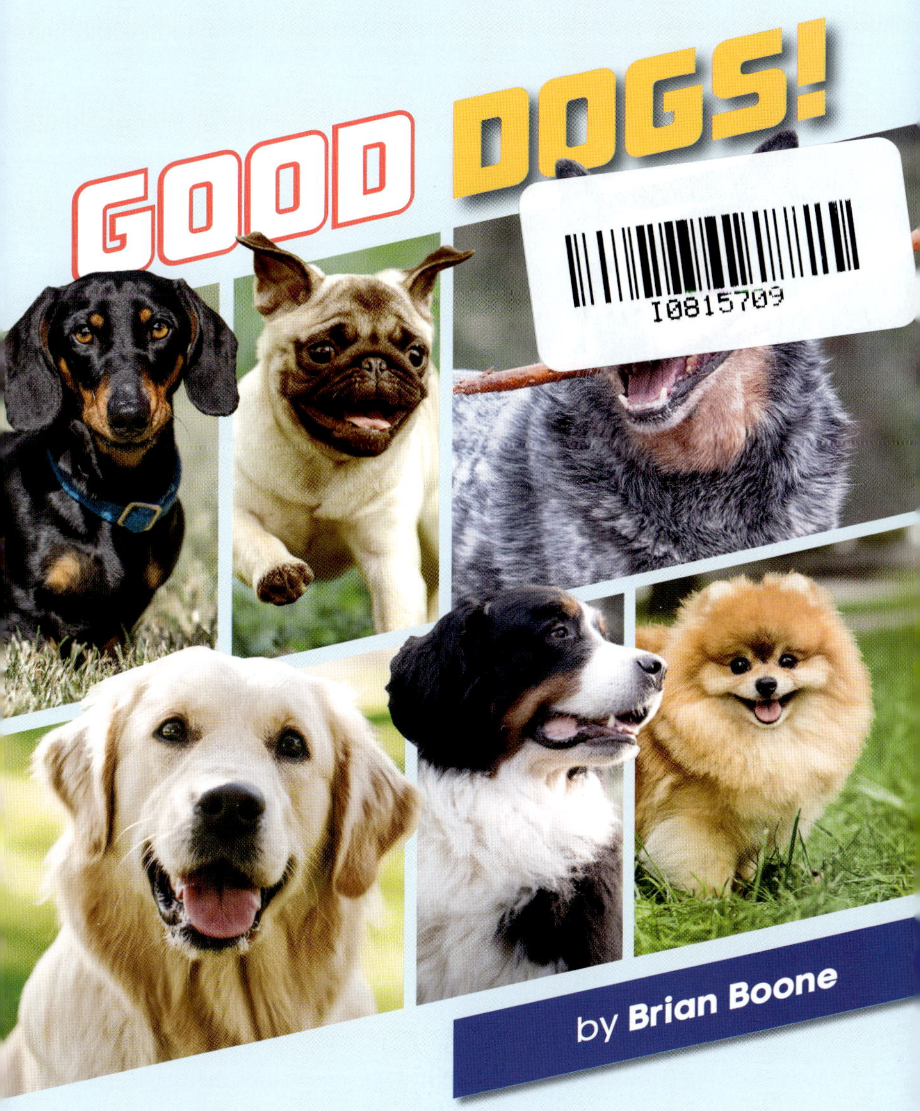

by **Brian Boone**

PENGUIN YOUNG READERS LICENSES
An imprint of Penguin Random House LLC
1745 Broadway, New York, NY 10019
penguinrandomhouse.com

Design by Leilani Abdur-Razzaq and Alice Wang

Library of Congress Cataloging-in-Publication Data is available.

First published in the United States of America by Penguin Young Readers Licenses,
an imprint of Penguin Random House LLC, 2026

Manufactured in China
TOPL

ISBN 9798217141838
10 9 8 7 6 5 4 3 2 1

Photo credits, all from Getty Images: cover: (background) shuang paul wang/iStock, (dachshund) chrisuk1/iStock, (pug) Alfredas Pliadis/iStock, (blue heeler) rdonar/iStock, (golden retriever) gorodenkoff/iStock, (Bernese mountain dog) Emilia Lepisto/iStock, (Pomeranian) romaset/iStock, (tennis ball) Azure-Dragon/iStock, (Pembroke Welsh corgi) DebbiSmirnoff/iStock, (English bulldog) feedough/iStock, (dalmatian) s5iztok/E+; 1: (dachshund) chrisuk1/iStock, (pug) Alfredas Pliadis/iStock, (blue heeler) rdonar/iStock, (golden retriever) gorodenkoff/iStock, (Bernese mountain dog) Emilia Lepisto/iStock, (Pomeranian) romaset/iStock; 2–3: AsyaPozniak/iStock; 5: Sergey Ryumin/Moment; 6: Image Source/DigitalVision; 7: (top) Julia_Siomuha/iStock, (bottom) cynoclub/iStock; 8: kitthanes/iStock; 9: (top) THEPALMER/iStock, (bottom) Berk Ucak/iStock; 10: (top) Cavan Images/iStock, (bottom) GlobalP/iStock; 11: (top) carlofranco/iStock, (bottom) Richard Bailey/Corbis Documentary; 12: cynoclub/iStock; 13: 4FR/iStock; 14: Sandra Schmid/Moment; 15: (top) IzaLysonArts / 500px/500px, (bottom) BananaStock/BananaStock; 16–17: Maryna Terletska/Moment; 18: GlobalP/iStock; 19: (top) Agency Animal Picture/Stockbyte, (bottom) oxygen/Moment; 20: (top) GlobalP/iStock, (bottom) Chris Amaral/DigitalVision; 21: (top) cynoclub/iStock, (bottom) Anita Kot/Moment; 22: (top) Bigandt_Photography/iStock, (bottom) Westend61/Westend61; 23: GlobalP/iStock; 24: (top) BestSide/iStock, (bottom) Robert Nieznanski/iStock; 25: @Hans Surfer/Moment; 26: Westend61/Westend61; 27: keita Somerville/iStock; 28: (top) Sima_ha/iStock, (bottom) Mariia Kokorina/iStock; 29: (top) master1305/iStock, (bottom) Peter König/500px; 30: Guy Cali/The Image Bank; 31: Olena Malik/Moment; 32: Anderson Leung / 500px/500px; 33: (top) GlobalP/iStock, (bottom) Anna Averianova / 500px/500px Prime; 34–35: Vsevolod Vlasenko/Moment; 36: (top) Martin Barraud/Stone, (bottom) Pavel Fedosseyev / 500px/500px; 37: (top) Bigandt_Photography/iStock, (bottom) ValerijaP/iStock; 38: (top) Andrew_Howe/E+, (bottom) GlobalP/iStock; 39: (top) Tetra Images/Tetra images, (bottom) GlobalP/iStock; 40: PavelRodimov/iStock; 41: Wirestock/iStock; 42–43: albertobrian/iStock; 44: JWB Fotografie/iStock; 45: SashaFoxWalters/iStock; 46–47: Zheka-Boss/iStock; 48: (top) RugliG/iStock, (bottom) JZHunt/iStock; 49: (top) Wirestock/iStock, (bottom) Liliya Kulianionak/iStock; 50: Wavetop/iStock; 51: (top) Svetlana Evgrafova/iStock, (bottom) alkir/iStock; 52: Richard Bailey/Corbis Documentary; 53: Stefan Cristian Cioata/Moment; 54: Eudyptula/iStock; 55: GlobalP/iStock; 56: DevidDO/iStock; 57: adogslifephoto/iStock; 58: Ekaterina Vakhrusheva/iStock; 59: Anita Kot/Moment; 60: Agency Animal Picture/Stockbyte; 61: cynoclub/iStock; 62: Anna Maloverjan / 500px/500Px Plus; 63: lukajani/E+; 64–65: olgagorovenko/iStock; 66–67: PopoudinaSvetlana/iStock; 68: master1305/iStock; 69: LynMc42k/iStock; 70–71: jermzlee/RooM; 72: Tatyana Consaul/iStock; 73: AsyaPozniak/iStock; 74: (top) Anita Kot/Moment, (bottom) DIMITAR DILKOFF / Contributor/AFP; 75: (top) Genaro Molina / Contributor/Los Angeles Times, (bottom) bruev/iStock; 76: fotojagodka/iStock; 77: UlrikeStein/iStock; 78: Abramova_Kseniya/iStock; 79: (top) Edwin_Butter/iStock, (bottom) GlobalP/iStock; 80: kostya6969/iStock; 81: pankration/E+; 82–83: Irina Vaneeva/iStock; 84: Sue Thatcher/iStock; 85: (top) Iza Łysoń/500px, (bottom) CaptureLight/iStock; 86: Cavan Images/Cavan; 87: feedough/iStock; 88: Brighton Dog Photography/Moment; 89: GlobalP/iStock; 90: Gary Padgett / 500px/500px; 91: Gordey Chadny/iStock; 92: GlobalP/iStock; 93: Olena Ruban/Moment; 94: Capuski/E+

CONTENTS

INTRODUCTION

Have you ever heard the expression "Dogs are man's best friend"? This means that canines, pooches, pups—*Canis lupus familiaris* (that's their scientific name)—are the treasured companions of many humans across the globe. Wherever and whenever people have lived on Earth, dogs have lived right along with them.

Lots of different types, or "breeds," of dogs were developed all over the world to help humans complete certain jobs. Originally, this was because dogs work very hard, can be trained, and are good at a variety of tasks. They helped people survive by finding food, assisting on farms, and protecting them. But dogs are also very cute and charming and have so much personality that all of humanity just fell in love with them. We made dogs our pets, our companions, and our friends.

There are so many kinds of dogs, and they're all unique and special in their own way. From big dogs to small dogs, to popular dogs to uncommon dogs, they're all here in this book. Inside you'll find frankly fascinating and doggone delightful facts about 101 dog types. You'll learn more about your favorites and may find some new ones, too.

AFGHAN HOUND

Nicknamed "the King of Dogs," the **AFGHAN HOUND** was first depicted in prehistoric cave drawings found in Afghanistan. According to legends about this breed, the Afghan hound was the one dog rescued from the biblical flood braved by Noah's ark. Thought to have been bred to hunt deer and leopards, Afghan hounds can reach speeds as high as forty miles per hour. Today, they're a luxury pet, with long, flowing, silky hair and a curly, pointy tail. Because of a very agile neck and a long and narrow head, the Afghan hound possesses a 270-degree field of vision.

AIREDALE TERRIER

Terrier is Latin for "of the land," and it refers to dogs once utilized to hunt and work on farms. The **AIREDALE TERRIER** is the largest terrier breed, weighing as much as sixty pounds. Bred in England to chase small animals, speedy Airedales were used as mail dogs during World War I. American troops brought them back to the US, and in the 1920s, they were the most popular dog in the country. President Warren G. Harding had one named Laddie Boy.

AKITA

Originating in the snowy mountains of Japan's Akita Prefecture (a district of Japan), the **AKITA** can climb steep and slippery peaks thanks to its muscular legs and two layers of fur. In ancient Japan, only rulers were allowed to have the Akita as a pet, but it has since become a beloved symbol of good luck and good health. Tiny statues are given to expectant mothers. No Akita ever left Japan until 1937, when the famed Helen Keller brought one to the United States, where it soon became a popular pet.

ALASKAN MALAMUTE

A pack animal and a working dog that needs to stay busy, the **ALASKAN MALAMUTE** can weigh as much as one hundred pounds. Perfect for surviving icy conditions, the Alaskan malamute has a double layer of fur to protect it from the snow, and a black nose that won't get sunburned by the light reflecting off the snow. The malamute was the sled dog used on the earliest expeditions to the North Pole and the South Pole after it was discovered living with Native communities in Alaska. Filmmaker George Lucas's malamute was the inspiration for the *Star Wars* character Chewbacca.

AMERICAN BULLDOG

When Western Europeans migrated to the United States in the 1800s, they brought their special dogs that were descended from English bulldogs. These became known as **AMERICAN BULLDOGS**. Farmers used them as guard dogs, as ratcatchers, and especially in the South, for running down and retrieving escaped pigs. These dogs are so named because they do what was once called bully work—tough outdoor labor. They were so valued in the South that the American bulldog was once called the White English Southern bulldog.

AMERICAN ESKIMO

This dog is a version of the spitz, brought to the United States with German immigrants in the late 1800s. Following World War I, when the United States had fought Germany, the American Kennel Club officially gave it the name **AMERICAN ESKIMO**, after a breeder called the American Eskimo Kennel, to separate the breed from its German roots. These dogs are quite playful, holding on to the mindset of a puppy for two years, which is about six months longer than most other dogs.

AMERICAN FOXHOUND

The **AMERICAN FOXHOUND** was one of the earliest dogs to be developed in what is now the United States. Hunting dogs brought from England were bred with French and Irish hounds to make for a dog that was fast, compact, and had a lot of stamina. George Washington owned and used one for hunting because these dogs have an incredible ability to track scents. Notable features of the American foxhound include its white, black, and tan fur; its big brown eyes; and its uniquely long bark.

AMERICAN STAFFORDSHIRE TERRIER

Long ago, the original version of this dog was used in violent wild animal–baiting games in England. After these dogs came to the United States in the late 1800s, they remained dense, compact, and strong, and larger than England's Staffordshire bull terrier but much calmer and sweeter. Today, **AMERICAN STAFFORDSHIRE TERRIERS**—also called AmStaffs—are popular family pets and considered devoted dogs. In 1903, an AmStaff named Bud was taken on the first-ever cross-country car trip. The most decorated hero dog of World War I was an AmStaff known as Sgt. Stubby.

AMERICAN WATER SPANIEL

Even though the **AMERICAN WATER SPANIEL** was developed in the Midwestern United States in the late 1800s, only about three thousand of them can be found in the country today. This descendant of the old English water spaniel was designed to hunt in both land and water. Its thick, wavy coat of chocolate-colored fur provides warmth in icy air and lakes, so they can swim out to boats to fetch whatever hunters have collected. Even though there aren't many individuals of this breed, it is so important to Wisconsin that it's the official dog of that state.

ANATOLIAN SHEPHERD DOG

Hailing from Anatolia, which is part of Turkey, this working dog is perfectly suited for hot summers and harsh winters. The **ANATOLIAN SHEPHERD DOG** is one of the world's biggest dogs, as adult males weigh about 150 pounds and stand three feet tall, and it is considered both speedy and strong. Sweet and easygoing with their human families, these canines originally worked as guard dogs, protecting flocks of sheep from wild predators. Their short coats require a lot of brushing, even though they shed all of it twice a year.

APPENZELLER SENNENHUND

Sennenhund is German for "mountain dog," and these double-coated, tricolored, long-tongued dogs are one of a particular class of dogs that was developed to work and play around the Alps of Switzerland. It's also known as the Appenzell cattle dog, which hints at how it's been historically utilized in Europe as a cattle herder. **APPENZELLER SENNENHUNDS** are good-natured, energetic, and loyal, which makes these dogs great for family pets, so long as they have plenty of room to run.

AUSTRALIAN CATTLE DOG

Australians in the 1800s needed an animal to drive cattle across large expanses of land, so they crossed the blue merle with the wolflike dingo and got the **AUSTRALIAN CATTLE DOG**. These dogs are more commonly known as blue or red heelers because their coats are silvery blue or red, and they gently bite the heels of cattle to guide them. Bluey from the popular TV show *Bluey* is a blue heeler.

AUSTRALIAN SHEPHERD

European people who worked as shepherds moved to Australia in the 1800s and brought their sheep and sheepdogs with them. The rugged dogs thrived in the much harsher Australian weather and terrain, with stamina to spare. When those dogs came to the United States, they acquired the name **AUSTRALIAN SHEPHERD**. They quickly grew popular as pets thanks to their fluffy white chests and luxurious, patchy coats of brown, white, and black. These dogs were often used in rodeo performances and Western movies in the mid-twentieth century, and most Australian shepherds today can have their lineages traced to those entertainment dogs.

BASENJI

Most all dogs bark, but the **BASENJI** does not. Because of a uniquely shaped voice box, it physically can't. When it needs to communicate, it instead wails, whines, and even yodels. The basenji also stands apart from other dogs thanks to its catlike qualities. They're known to be independent and often groom themselves, similar to cats. This breed is possibly the world's oldest known dog breed. These small but tough animals used to help hunt lions in central Africa, and they were often brought to ancient Egypt as gifts for pharaohs.

BASSET HOUND

This dog is instantly identified by its sleepy expression and short legs. The **BASSET HOUND'S** oversize drooping ears are among the longest in the dog world. Popular in the United States since the 1950s, basset hounds were initially developed by French royals to be used during rabbit hunts—their low noses can easily pick up a scent, and their dragging ears collect it, too, providing a constant reminder for the basset hound as it continues to search. Their white-tipped tails make them easier to spot from far away when they're tracking in tall grass and thick underbrush.

BEAGLE

It's no surprise that **BEAGLES** are so good at making friends when you look into their big, sweet eyes. Beagles are hounds, trained since the Middle Ages to chase down rabbits. It's unclear where exactly they came from, but what is clear is that these dogs love to bark, howl, and use their large collection of different sounds that all have different meanings. If those floppy ears look familiar, it's because one of the most famous fictional dogs in the world is a beagle: Snoopy!

BEARDED COLLIE

Frequently confused with other shaggy dogs, the **BEARDED COLLIE** has long light-colored hair that drapes over its face and covers its eyes. Bearded collies love to jump and bounce to burn off energy. Friendly but stubborn, they need lots of attention and playtime or else they can grow anxious. A favorite of Hollywood, bearded collies starred in movies like *The Shaggy Dog* (2006) and TV shows like *The Brady Bunch*.

BERGAMASCO SHEEPDOG

The **BERGAMASCO SHEEPDOG** features ropey braids that drape all over its face, body, and tail. Amazingly, those mats don't get dirty, even if the Bergamasco is doing the outdoors job it was bred to do: protect sheep. It was originally called the Alpine sheepdog because it assisted shepherds in the mountains of Europe by guarding flocks at night. When a shepherd from Bergamo, Italy, adopted a few of these dogs, they quickly became popular there, and the name changed to the Italian one it has today. Their noteworthy locks offer protection: If a predator lunges at them, they'll get a mouthful of hair rather than flesh.

BERNESE MOUNTAIN DOG

When Roman armies moved into the mountains of Bern, Switzerland, two thousand years ago, they brought mastiffs with them, which farmers then bred with a local longhaired herding dog. The descendant became the **BERNESE MOUNTAIN DOG**, which is as friendly as it is helpful. Their hair is long and silky to withstand cold temperatures. They've got a lot of energy and a will to work, so farmers traditionally used them to pull carts—they can drag up to a thousand pounds, which is more than ten times their weight.

BICHON FRISE

The **BICHON FRISE** is the kind of dog that loves to be close to its owner and carried around. That goes back to King Henry III of France, who used to show off his bichon frise dogs in a basket he wore around his neck during the sixteenth century. A cross between a poodle and a water spaniel, the bichon frise's ancestors were hunters. The bichon frise, however, has never been a hunter and is instead a loyal companion. They later appeared as circus dogs because they can be trained to do tricks. Some owners claim that these small white dogs smile when they are happy.

BLOODHOUND

The **BLOODHOUND** is known for having the longest, droopiest face; heavy eyelids; and long, floppy ears to match. This canine stems from big hunting hounds that were brought from Belgium to England in the eleventh century. Bloodhounds earned their name because of the phrase "blooded" hound. "Blooded" is what people used to call a dog that was of pure breeding. Bloodhounds are helpful to humans because of their powerful sense of smell.

BOERBOEL

Dutch, German, and French settlers and farmers, known as Boers, colonized South Africa in the 1800s. They needed big dogs to protect their remote homes and crops from wild animals, particularly lions and baboon packs. They bred their giant mastiffs with various varieties of African native dogs to create the **BOERBOEL**. Strong enough to scare off a lion and fast enough to chase off baboons, these massive dogs can weigh as much as two hundred pounds. Despite their origin as tough guys, they're calm and obedient when they're not working.

BORDER COLLIE

Beyond the soft coat, these energetic and athletic dogs are quite literally bright-eyed and bushy-tailed. They need lots of activity—which is why they have dominated so many herding trials and agility competitions. Cited by some studies as the smartest dog, the **BORDER COLLIE** first originated in Great Britain from livestock-guarding dogs brought by Roman invaders. They were later bred with the Vikings' spitzes. That created a hardy field dog. These canines then crept, snuck, and pounced around in the fields of Scotland and England for centuries to come.

BORDER TERRIER

The *border* in **BORDER TERRIER** refers to the physical border of the hills between England and Scotland. This is where these dogs were first bred and put to work. The sheep-thieving hill fox once tormented the area, and the border terrier had the speed to chase these critters off. Maxing out at sixteen inches tall and fifteen pounds, border terriers are small enough to dig into fox holes and chase their target. The border terrier is uniquely adept at getting out of entanglements and, despite their little legs, climbing walls.

BOSTON TERRIER

Horse-drawn carriage drivers in Boston in the 1860s bred their bulldogs and terriers with their bosses' fancier purebred dogs. That created this pointy-eared pooch with the black-and-white face and body. Goofy and affectionate, this dog's face rests in a permanent smile and its markings resemble a tuxedo, which is how it gained the nickname "the American Gentleman." The **BOSTON TERRIER'S** short muzzle makes it hard for it to breathe, and the dog tends to swallow air while it eats due to its distinct head shape. Because of this, the Boston terrier often grunts, snorts, snores, and farts.

BOXER

No dog has a longer tongue than the **BOXER**—the record holder measured almost six inches. With an energy like that of a toddler, boxers are very playful. They'll stand on their hind legs to play, jump, and box. One can tell a boxer is happy because it'll wag its entire rear end, as boxers usually have stubby tails. This dog's short nose and smushed-in face was a desirable trait for hunters who wanted a dog that could easily hold and carry its prey.

BOYKIN SPANIEL

Bred in South Carolina to assist duck hunters on rivers, the **BOYKIN SPANIEL** is nicknamed "the dog that doesn't rock the boat"—they're too little to make much motion when they jump in, unlike other hunting dogs. One of the newest dog breeds in the world, the Boykin spaniel is the result of two stray dogs that were bred around 1905, named Dumpy and Singo. It's such a treasured dog in South Carolina that it's the state's official dog, and September 1 is Boykin Spaniel Day.

BRAQUE SAINT-GERMAIN

When a kennel from Compiegne, France, moved to Saint-Germain, France, in the 1800s, the Compiegne pointer acquired a new name—the **BRAQUE SAINT-GERMAIN**—to fit its new home. This dog is a mix of the familiar pointer and the rare Braque Francais. With a stripe down its head and a white or spotted coat on the body, this dog can easily blend into its natural surroundings while hunting. It became more popular around France through word of mouth as French game hunters talked up the Braque Saint-Germain as a loyal and effective companion.

BULL TERRIER

Most recognizable for their egg-shaped heads, **BULL TERRIERS** are emotional, often veering between silly and stubborn. They're very smart and also need to exercise a lot. They're also strong and speedy, getting strength from the bulldogs and zippiness from terriers. General George Patton took his with him to the front lines of World War II. This makes sense because bull terriers are often trained to do specific jobs, such as bomb detection, search-and-rescue, and therapy. Target's mascot, Bullseye, is a bull terrier.

BULLDOG

Bulldogs can be traced to the thirteenth century, where it is believed that they were used for bullbaiting—a medieval sport where a dog was set loose to attack a tethered bull. They were later rehabilitated in the 1800s to become sweet companions and to star in the brand-new phenomenon of dog shows. They may look angry, but experts say **BULLDOGS** are some of the friendliest dogs around. Two presidents have owned bulldogs—Calvin Coolidge and Warren G. Harding.

BULLMASTIFF

In the late nineteenth century, there was an uptick in animal burglaries among England's country estates and game preserves. In response, gamekeepers bred new dogs that were strong, brave, and willing to chase intruders through the fields at night. They combined the two biggest and toughest dogs of the era—mastiffs from the mountains of Europe and bulldogs. The **BULLMASTIFF**, still nicknamed "the Gamekeeper's Night Dog," is generally kind to all except its target enemy, and it can strike fear, too: It is two feet tall but can weigh a whopping 130 pounds.

CAIRN TERRIER

This tiny dog—ten inches tall and fifteen inches long at most—ran all over the rocky Highlands of Scotland for two hundred years before anyone gave the breed an official name. These surprisingly strong dogs love to dig, and they were once valued for hunting foxes and other pests in their hideout holes. They gained their name because they easily hunted rats, which would hide under land-marking stone piles called cairns. In 1939, a **CAIRN TERRIER** named Terry became a major movie star—he played Toto in *The Wizard of Oz*.

CANE CORSO

When the Molossians of ancient Greece were taken over by the Roman Republic, they brought dogs that were almost as big as horses. When these massive dogs were bred with native breeds, the result was the **CANE CORSO**. They were used by Roman soldiers to charge into enemy lines, carrying buckets of flaming oil. After the fall of Rome, they guarded livestock and henhouses. Very territorial and protective, the cane corso has a stiff coat that barely hides the bulging muscles beneath. The name *cane corso* translates to "bodyguard dog," which is fitting for this loyal hound.

CAVALIER KING CHARLES SPANIEL

European royal families bred dogs to be fashionable accessories and shows of wealth in the 1600s, and English kings Charles I and Charles II loved this floppy-eared breed so much that the dog was named in their honor. The **CAVALIER KING CHARLES SPANIEL** remained an elite favorite throughout the 1800s, and breeders crossed them with other tiny dogs to make even more delicate pets. These canines come in four color variations: chestnut and white; black, white, and tan; black and tan; and red.

CHIHUAHUA

The smallest dog ever, the **CHIHUAHUA** is named after its home region in Mexico, where nobles treasured these dogs for friendship and warmth. One of the oldest dogs from the Americas, some experts think that the first Chihuahuas might have descended from foxes. It is also one of the only dogs with a molera, a soft spot on the top of its head that never hardens. Those ears that stick straight up might be cute, but they're actually useful tools that help the Chihuahua regulate body temperature and listen for sounds of predators.

CHINESE SHAR-PEI

You might recognize this breed as the dog that's covered in thick, rough wrinkles everywhere. These interesting wrinkles are actually important and are meant to keep the dogs' organs protected. That feature was bred into the dog two thousand years ago in China, where shar-pei dogs worked as palace guardians. Their unique blue-black tongue was said to keep away evil spirits. It was little known in the United States until 1979, when one was pictured on the cover of *Life* magazine that year, launching a huge rise in the **CHINESE SHAR-PEI** as an American house pet.

CHINOOK

New Hampshire man Arthur Walden went to Alaska in the 1890s and worked as a sled dog driver, then returned home with the goal to create the perfect friendly dog for that task. He bred a husky with a mastiff and named the new variety after his lead sled dog, **CHINOOK** (which is the name of a Pacific Northwest Indigenous community). There are only about 1,200 Chinook in the world, but it's the beloved state dog of New Hampshire.

CHOW CHOW

When the Han dynasty ruled China around 200 BC, **CHOW CHOWS** were the favorite dog of the nobility; when the Tang dynasty took over, one emperor was said to have loved chow chows so much that he raised five thousand of them. Their name is an accident. When British traders returned from China with these dogs in the eighteenth century, they were listed in a boat's cargo load as "chow chow," which is a phrase that means "various" or "et cetera." First displayed at the London Zoo in the 1820s, Britons adopted chow chows as family pets in big numbers after Queen Victoria adopted one.

COCKER SPANIEL

Spaniels are hunting dogs, and when English researchers started classifying this type in the nineteenth century, they named this one the **COCKER SPANIEL** because it specialized in tracking a specific bird called the woodcock. The American version of the English cocker spaniel exploded when Brucie won two Westminster Dog Shows back-to-back in the 1940s. Then one was featured in *Lady and the Tramp* in 1955. Throughout the 1950s, more American households had cocker spaniels than any other dog.

COLLIE

In the mid-twentieth century, books, movies, and TV shows about a smart, heroic dog named Lassie put the **COLLIE** on the map. The devoted and protective Lassie was a pretty accurate portrayal of the breed. In 1923, a collie named Bobbie walked from Indiana to Oregon to find her family after she was lost on vacation. Collies were originally developed in the hillsides of Wales and Scotland to be herders and helpers. These canines are famously covered in long, flowing, multicolored hair that once protected them from the cold and rainy weather.

DACHSHUND

About six hundred years ago, badger hunters in Germany needed a dog that was long, slim, and close to the ground to invade burrows. *Dachshund* translates to "badger dog," but it's commonly referred to as a "wiener dog" due to the dog's signature tubular, sausage-shaped body. While **DACHSHUNDS** seem cute, they can weigh in at a dense thirty-two pounds and possess some of the sharpest teeth and claws found in dogs. These suited them well for hunting. They're so loved in Germany that they are a national symbol of the country.

DALMATIAN

Tall and lanky, this dog was made unforgettable by the 1961 movie *101 Dalmatians*. The **DALMATIAN** is recognizable by its white fur with black spots. Those famous markings are everywhere, even on its underbelly and the inside of its mouth. Dalmatians were used in nineteenth-century England to run alongside horse-drawn coaches to clear out crowds of people to make a path for the horses. That led to a similar job with fire trucks, and today they're still a common firehouse dog.

DOBERMAN PINSCHER

German tax collector Louis Dobermann needed a dog to ward off bandits as he went about his business in the late 1800s. For this reason, he took a dog from a German line of dogs called pinschers and set about mixing in the genes of other dogs (precisely which breeds remains unknown) to get a dog that was smart, fast, tough, and loyal, but only to its owner. Dobermann's **DOBERMAN PINSCHERS** also became strong and muscular, solidly built with a thick head, making them a favorite animal for the military and for police K-9 units around the United States.

DOGUE DE BORDEAUX

The word *dog* comes from *dogue*, a French word for muscular mastiffs like the **DOGUE DE BORDEAUX**. More than just heavy canines (they weigh about one hundred pounds), these dogs also boast the biggest heads of any dog in the world. After the French Revolution eliminated the country estates that the Dogue had once guarded, they soon became cart pullers for butchers. The Dogue de Bordeaux stayed nearly unknown beyond France until 1989, when a cranky, slobbering one starred in the hit movie *Turner and Hooch.*

DREVER

This breed is obscure in most countries except Sweden, where the government declared the rare **DREVER** a national treasure in 1953. Bred from Germany's Westphalian Dachsbracke since 1910, the Drever's traits and abilities helped rural communities hunt and eat. With an excellent nose for tracking, the Drever has the low, long body and strong legs needed to find deer in forests and chase them long distances, away from adjacent livestock-grazing areas.

ENGLISH FOXHOUND

Many dog experts count the **ENGLISH FOXHOUND** among the most naturally friendly dogs. Oddly, these dogs are almost never kept as pets: They're pack animals and have lived alongside one another for more than three hundred years. The English foxhound is one of the few dogs that still does the job it was bred to do, which is to team up and chase down foxes. Initially trained to get rid of pesky, chicken coop–raiding foxes, the English foxhound was eventually absorbed into the sport of fox hunting.

ENGLISH SETTER

The **ENGLISH SETTER** made a name for itself in the hilly, wide-open field areas of northern England in the 1300s. Tasked with tracking birds, these dogs catch a scent and chase it down. When they locate their target, they'll crouch, or "set," in place, in its direction. In the 1800s, English breeder Edward Laverack set about perfecting the breed, and he named the dog's distinctive coat pattern "belton" in honor of his favorite town. Its coat is white with flecks or waves of dark brown. It hangs long and loosely over a tall and lean body.

ENGLISH SPRINGER SPANIEL

Putting its stellar sense of smell to use, the springer spaniel once assisted bird hunters in the 1500s. This dog would find ducks and geese in tall grass and then "spring," startling the birds into flying away. This made it easier for hunters to target the birds. Various types of **ENGLISH SPRINGER SPANIELS** developed, including the Norfolk spaniel, which was developed by the Duke of Norfolk. This breed was renamed the English springer spaniel in 1900. Today, its nose and ability to communicate a location makes it very attractive for search-and-rescue efforts conducted by police departments.

ESTRELA MOUNTAIN DOG

The **ESTRELA MOUNTAIN DOG** has been herding sheep in Portugal for at least a thousand years. This strong, agile, and fiercely protective dog is likely a mix of local breeds with dogs brought by invading Romans and Visigoths. Unknown outside of that one remote region of Portugal until the twentieth century, Estrela mountain dogs aren't used much for protecting flocks anymore, but the service and companionship they provide are still important—they're among the most popular police dogs and family pets in that country.

FINNISH SPITZ

The Suomenpystykorva, literally "**FINNISH SPITZ**," came to Finland from Russia about three thousand years ago. Sometimes this dog is mistaken for a fox. It's got a face and reddish coat like that of a fox, but this hound is unmistakably a dog with its big bark. Trained and bred to be a hunting dog, the Finnish spitz barks loudly and repeatedly to let its human companions know when it has found something. Now, many remaining Finnish spitzes are employed as very capable alert dogs. Barking competitions are held around Finland to identify the Finnish spitz with the best of that noteworthy behavior.

FLAT-COATED RETRIEVER

Black or chocolate-colored hair lies stiff across most of the **FLAT-COATED RETRIEVER**, but its hair resembles feathers around its legs and tail. In fact, the tail of this dog is one of the biggest and most active among dogs. Flat-coated retrievers are scientifically proven to be one of the happiest dogs in the world, which is connected to how they keep a puppylike, playful attitude throughout their entire lives. These dogs are also great swimmers and can mentally mark a spot in water to retrieve their target, then swim right to it.

FRENCH BULLDOG

When the lacework industry moved from England to France in the 1800s, the women who worked in lacemaking brought along their dogs. These canines were small mixes of English bulldogs and terriers. From then on known as **FRENCH BULLDOGS**, they are not the most rugged creatures. Short heads and short noses cause French bulldogs trouble with breathing, so they can't play or swim for too long. Their short airways also lead to a lot of snorting and snarling, and they can sometimes sound similar to pigs.

GERMAN LONGHAIRED POINTER

Known in German as the Deutsch Langhaar, this dog is a pointer—when this pooch with a well-tuned nose finds what it's looking for, it stops and points its whole body in the direction of the target. Back in the 1800s, that target was usually a type of waterfowl, as hunters often took these dogs along to find and then retrieve ducks and geese. **GERMAN LONGHAIRED POINTERS** are built for that, too, with their thick overcoats and shorter undercoats that keep them warm when they dive into rivers and lakes.

GERMAN SHEPHERD DOG

These strong, tall-eared, majestic dogs were enlisted into service by the German military beginning in 1899. After World War I, American soldiers liked the German shepherd so much, they brought some back to the United States as pets. In the 1920s, adventure movies starring a rescue dog named Rin-Tin-Tin made him one of the biggest celebrities of the decade and increased the popularity of this breed. Today, more than eight thousand **GERMAN SHEPHERD DOGS** work in the United States, mostly for police departments because they can speedily run down suspects and can be trained to uncover explosives and illegal substances such as drugs.

GOLDEN RETRIEVER

Beloved in the United States since they first gained popularity in the 1930s, the **GOLDEN RETRIEVER** is the ideal family dog. This big breed is well-behaved, too. They don't bark much, and they have what's called a "soft mouth"—which means they can carry raw eggs in their mouths without breaking them. Many think this proves just how gentle these sunny canines truly are. In the 1860s, British lord Tweedmouth created the breed to be a water-hunting companion. Golden retrievers are good at following orders and they often excel in dog sports competitions like obedience, agility, and dock diving.

GREAT DANE

The tallest dog on Earth, the **GREAT DANE** stands more than six feet tall on its hind legs. No one is quite sure why this massive breed is called the Great Dane, because it's from Germany, not Denmark. In the past, these dogs used their strength and speed to serve as patrol dogs. These now docile dogs are big lap-sitters, a far cry from their use in medieval times, when their intimidating presence was said to scare off evil ghosts!

GREAT PYRENEES

Named after the mountains in France where it once roamed, the **GREAT PYRENEES** is a gentle giant of pure white fur. This massive dog originated in central Asia and migrated to Europe five thousand years ago. They once guarded sheep because they're naturally nurturing toward animals smaller than themselves. This special breed is also nocturnal. The Great Pyrenees can walk long distances and over mountains thanks to its extra claws on its hind legs. They were used in World War II to secretly transport cargo across the mountains.

GREATER SWISS MOUNTAIN DOG

The **GREATER SWISS MOUNTAIN DOG** comes from a line of muscular Metzerhund, which is a dog similar to a modern-day rottweiler. This breed went to work for food producers because it can haul a cart with as much as three thousand pounds of cargo, such as heavy jars of milk or big wheels of cheese. By 1900, motorized vehicles made this dog less important as a work-dog, and the breed slowly began to die out until the Swiss Army used them as pulling dogs during World War II.

GREYHOUND

Tall, narrow, and muscular, **GREYHOUNDS** are so aerodynamic that it's no wonder they're considered the best racing dogs. Elegant and swift with thick, soft pads on their feet, these dogs can run for short distances or long ones. Possessing one of the most unique dog bodies, the greyhound takes on the shape of a backward S. These canines were often the subject of paintings during the Italian Renaissance—when they weren't sitting beside the monarchs of Europe.

IRISH SETTER

After an **IRISH SETTER** was gifted to President Richard Nixon in 1968, the dog's popularity skyrocketed in the United States. Bred in the 1700s throughout Ireland from various local spaniels and setters, this dog's singular silky, flowing reddish-brown coat was once white with just a little red, before their current pattern settled in the 1800s. Irish setters were used to help hunters find birds, and unlike ground-sniffing hounds, Irish setters can track a scent in the air. They then run in a jagged pattern to memorize it.

IRISH TERRIER

With its short, scruffy red coat, the small and wiry **IRISH TERRIER** was the farm dog of choice in Ireland from the seventeenth century onward. Despite the name, these natural ratcatchers may have originated in Scotland. They're one of the oldest known terriers. Naturally alert and good with other animals, these dogs earned various jobs from farmers, like keeping watch on the land and protecting flocks of sheep. Used as messengers during World War I, several of these canines were brought back by American troops to the United States, where they were a popular pet throughout the 1920s.

IRISH WOLFHOUND

According to Irish lore, fourth-century Roman statesman Quintus Aurelius Symmachus was gifted seven dogs, which he called "the Great Hounds of Ireland." Those great hounds are thought to have been **IRISH WOLFHOUNDS**. For centuries, it was established (and then made law in some places) that these gigantic specimens were fit for royal companions only, and powerful people in courts from all around Europe gave them to one another as gifts. Kings used Irish wolfhounds when hunting big game. These dogs were also dispatched for military use because they are so tall and strong, they were able to pull enemy troops off their horses.

KOMONDOR

Covered entirely in long, thick white cords that even cover their eyes, **KOMONDORS** are big dogs that stand more than two feet tall and weigh more than one hundred pounds thanks to their thick bones and big muscles. One wouldn't know that, though, by how effortlessly and lightly these canines trot along. They're alert and agile, which is important because they were bred in Hungary to protect sheep flocks from wolves. Their thick cords kept them warm and protected them from wolf bites.

LABRADOR RETRIEVER

An iconic family dog, the **LABRADOR RETRIEVER** is relaxed and laid-back. Its permanent smile conveys the friendliness and loyalty for which it is treasured. Found in yellow, black, or chocolate brown, these scruffy dogs aren't named after their land of origin—the province of Newfoundland and Labrador in Canada—but rather a nearby waterway called the Labrador Sea. These dogs were bred to be a smaller version of the Newfoundland breed in the early 1800s, and their purpose was to retrieve nets and stray fish for fishermen. The Labrador retriever's webbed paws and water-wicking, oily coat make them great swimmers.

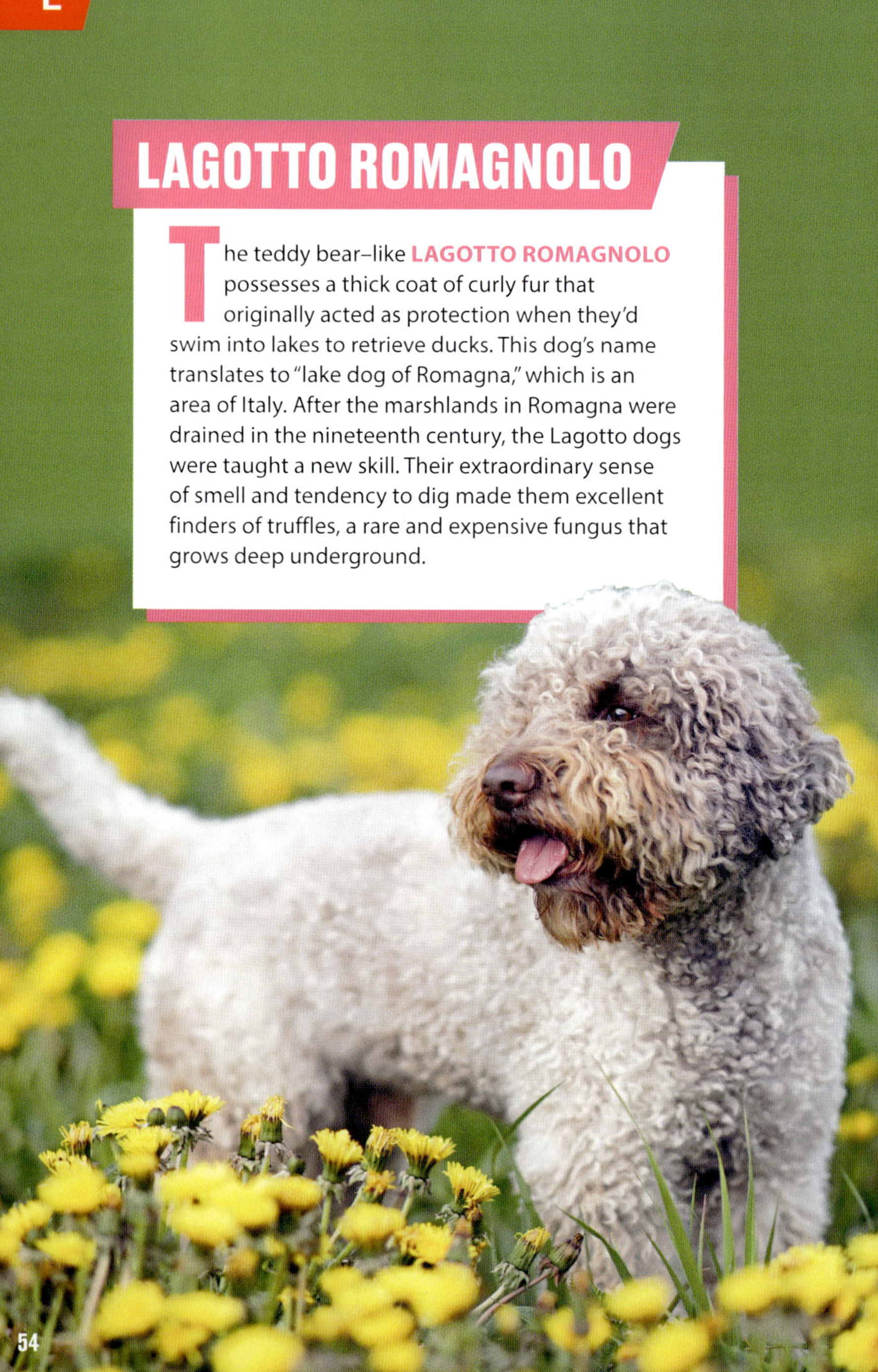

LAGOTTO ROMAGNOLO

The teddy bear–like **LAGOTTO ROMAGNOLO** possesses a thick coat of curly fur that originally acted as protection when they'd swim into lakes to retrieve ducks. This dog's name translates to "lake dog of Romagna," which is an area of Italy. After the marshlands in Romagna were drained in the nineteenth century, the Lagotto dogs were taught a new skill. Their extraordinary sense of smell and tendency to dig made them excellent finders of truffles, a rare and expensive fungus that grows deep underground.

LHASA APSO

The **LHASA APSO** has been around for a very long time. This long-haired breed originated in the Himalayas mountain system about 1,200 years ago. Lhasa apsos live long lives and frequently reach fifteen years of age. The oldest Lhasa apso on record lived to be twenty-nine years old! These dogs are on the smaller side and typically weigh between twelve and eighteen pounds.

MALTESE

Worshipped in ancient Egypt and depicted in ancient Greek art, these small white dogs have always been quite popular. The philosopher Aristotle likened this fluffy, button-nosed dog to "a cloud floating in the sky." For thousands of years, the **MALTESE** could be found in a number of colors, but in the twentieth century, a preference for all-white emerged among breeders and keepers. The Maltese originated as many as eight thousand years ago in Malta, an island country in the Mediterranean Sea, and was once a working dog before it became a status symbol for the rich. Today, the Maltese is the kind of dog you can carry around with you thanks to their tiny size.

MASTIFF

Likely the largest dog in history, the **MASTIFF** can weigh as much as 230 pounds because it is bulked up with heavy muscles and thick bones. This dog is considered the modern version of the Molosser, an extinct ancient Greek dog. The mastiff is a protector of land and people. When Roman soldiers invaded Britain in 55 BC, mastiffs helped defend the island. At the Battle of Agincourt in the fifteenth century, they were part of the English army that fought the French.

MINIATURE AMERICAN SHEPHERD

One of the newest dog types, the **MINIATURE AMERICAN SHEPHERD** dates back to the 1960s. Breeders from California wanted to make a smaller Australian shepherd, so they created a new kind of dog by breeding Aussies they found working as herding dogs at rodeos. These dogs retained the hardworking mindset of their relative, and they still share the same colorful and patchy coats. Miniature American shepherds are smaller and intended to be pets. Thanks to their rodeo origins, they also have a deep fondness for horses.

NEWFOUNDLAND

The massive **NEWFOUNDLAND** can weigh as much as 150 pounds. It is considered the biggest water dog and one of the largest dog breeds overall. This breed's strong legs, large lungs, and oily coats help them swim in cold waters for hours at a time. Their droopy face jowls create narrow airways to keep them breathing. Fishing crews working in and around Canada's province of Newfoundland and Labrador had their strong Newfies haul nets full of cod ashore. The most famous fictional Newfoundland is Nana, the gentle giant who watched over the kids in *Peter Pan*.

NORWEGIAN BUHUND

When Vikings raided European ports a thousand years ago, they brought along their **NORWEGIAN BUHUNDS**. The dogs even helped in the looting because they are loyal to their humans. After the Viking Age ended, Norwegian buhunds were put to use on the rainy coast of Norway for herding sheep on farms, and this is how they got their name. *Buhund* translates to "farm dog." Many dogs of this breed are still used for that purpose. The most famous dog in Norway is a buhund named Skip, who has a magazine column in which he demonstrates his tricks.

OLD ENGLISH SHEEPDOG

Very large even without all its shaggy, voluminous hair, the **OLD ENGLISH SHEEPDOG** was designed to direct cattle from the farm to the market. It earned its name because it's fluffy like a sheep. It is also called the bobtail because it has a very stubby tail under its fluffy coat. The Old English sheepdog emerged in England in the 1700s as a cross between Scottish and Russian dogs. These pups have inspired some notable characters in entertainment, such as the main character in Disney's *The Shaggy Dog* (1959) movie.

PAPILLON

Seen in many Italian paintings in the 1500s, this tiny dog was developed to occupy laps. It made its way to Spain and then France on the backs of mules in the 1600s. France's king Louis XIV was a fan of this breed, which is why its name is a French word. *Papillon* means "butterfly," and the dog is called this because its ears look like the wings of the flying insect. These dogs are historically cute, which is how they quickly became one of the most popular show dogs. In 1999, a **PAPILLON** from Connecticut named Kirby swept three major international dog shows: the Westminster Kennel Club Dog Show in the United Kingdom, the World Dog Show in Finland, and the Royal Canadian Show.

PARSON RUSSELL TERRIER

During the late 1800s in England, Parson John "Jack" Russell crossed different breeds of terriers to make a new dog that was uniquely suited to fox hunting. Also called the Jack Russell terrier, this dog can chase rabbits over land and also into their hiding holes. Nowadays, this scruffy-faced little dog is a bundle of energy. It'll spend its days jumping, barking, and running in circles. **PARSON RUSSELL TERRIERS** are naturally talented performers, which led to their use in film and classic TV shows such as *Frasier* and *Wishbone*.

PEMBROKE WELSH CORGI

Despite their short legs, **PEMBROKE WELSH CORGIS** are excellent dancers, and that's just one of the tricks they can be trained to do because of their above-average intelligence and confidence. In the twelfth century, Belgian migrants brought various small dogs with them to Pembrokeshire, Wales, and bred new herding dogs. This is how the corgi came to be. Corgis tell cows and sheep where to go by nipping at their heels. With fluffy, feathery coats, these big-eared, ground-level dogs are probably best known as the beloved companions of Queen Elizabeth II.

POMERANIAN

Pomeranians mimic the behavior of large dogs, which is a bit silly because **POMERANIANS** only weigh about seven pounds. This odd personality trait may be because these tiny dogs have Arctic sled dog ancestors. Those ancestors originated in Pomerania, which is now part of Poland and Germany. The wildly sprouting red-brown hair that Pomeranians have made them somewhat of a fashion accessory to wealthy nineteenth-century Europeans. Queen Victoria brought one back from Italy, and then they became very popular in England. Composer Wolfgang Amadeus Mozart and French queen Marie Antoinette also had Pomeranians as pets.

POODLE

There's no dog more famous for its haircut than the **POODLE**. The traditional haircut given to poodles includes round puffs of hair on a shaved body. These were thought to warm their joints as they swam in cold waters. Originating in Germany, the poodle gets its name from a German word that means "puddle," because poodles were hunting dogs used as water retrievers. The poodle comes in three distinct sizes: standard, miniature, and toy.

PORTUGUESE WATER DOG

Many centuries ago, fishers working off the coast of Portugal used these dogs as helpers. The **PORTUGUESE WATER DOG** could herd fish into a net, track down lost gear, and swim to other ships to deliver messages with ease. They'd even go along on deep-sea fishing trips because their coats made from tight curls would keep them warm for the entire journey between Portugal and Iceland. Once rare in the United States, the Portuguese water dog got a boost in popularity when President Barack Obama's family adopted two puppies named Bo and Sunny while he was in the White House.

PUG

Breeders in ancient China are said to have designed the **PUG** to have extra skin on its face that would form wrinkles replicating the Chinese characters for the word *prince*. These were the dogs of royals and the elite. The pug's eyes resemble big black marbles, and they bulge a bit out of its head. This dog's flat face means it has very small airways, so pugs usually have trouble breathing. This makes living in warm weather challenging for them.

RAT TERRIER

A terrier is a dog small enough to fit into holes in the ground, and the **RAT TERRIER** was designed in England to find and eliminate rats before they could destroy farm crops. These pied dogs (meaning they've got colored patches atop a white coat) are related to greyhounds and beagles, and the remains of one was found in 1981 on the sixteenth-century wreck of King Henry VIII's flagship the *Mary Rose*.

RHODESIAN RIDGEBACK

The Khoisan community in southern Africa is where the **RHODESIAN RIDGEBACK** was first developed. After Dutch and German settlers arrived in what was once called Rhodesia, the settlers bred their Great Danes and greyhounds with the semi-wild wolves used by the locals for the dangerous task of lion hunting. This dog has a large, muscular body with a ridge that runs down its entire back. With thickly padded and arched toes, the Rhodesian ridgeback can run alongside horses for many miles.

RESCUE DOGS

A lot of the dogs one encounters aren't just one breed—they've got several different types of dogs in their background, and that's why they have a collection of so many features found in several other dogs. These dogs are referred to as "mixed breeds." However, they're just as special as show dogs or a purebred dog with a carefully tracked background called a pedigree. **RESCUE DOGS** are one of a kind—and they're easy to find waiting for a "forever home" at a local dog shelter or animal welfare organization. Adopting a rescue dog is great for your community and helps homeless dogs find happy lives with loving families.

ROTTWEILER

This tough animal is a favorite for guard dog gigs. The **ROTTWEILER** is illegal to own in many countries because of its old reputation, but many rottweilers are incredibly sweet. While the breed used to be vicious, they're also very smart and can be trained to be anything from a loving family pet to a working dog. These big canines originated as herders and cart pullers in ancient Rome and were valued for their bite, too—they have one of the strongest jaws of any dog.

SAINT BERNARD

In the eleventh century, a monk (who later became a saint) named Bernard opened a hospice in the Swiss Alps to care for travelers braving the mountains. When those facilities began search-and-rescue efforts in the seventeenth century, they used massive dogs that had been developed over hundreds of years. This breed of dog became known as the **SAINT BERNARD**. They can find people buried under as much as twenty feet of snow, and they're expert diggers. It's estimated that these gentle giants have saved more than two thousand lives in the Swiss Alps.

SAMOYED

A thousand years ago, the Samoyede people migrated to Siberia, one of Earth's coldest regions. Their favored working dog, the **SAMOYED**, was able to pull one and a half times its own weight, herd reindeer, and even act as blankets at night to keep their owners warm. Arctic explorers in the eighteenth century brought some of these dogs back to Europe, while the rest stayed behind to pull the sleds used in North Pole expeditions. Their smiling, upturned mouths are that way for a reason: This cuts down on the amount of drool that drips from the Samoyed's mouth so that icicles won't form on its face in the cold weather.

SCHAPENDOES

A shaggy, fun-loving pet that loves to delight its humans, this one is also known as the Dutch sheepdog. Once common in the Netherlands as a farm dog, the arrival of the border collie in the twentieth century led to the **SCHAPENDOES** becoming a less common choice for farmers and families. Rare by 1947, a group dedicated to making schapendoes popular again brought them back. All schapendoes alive in the world today come from one family line that was established in the 1970s. They've got long hair and a bouncy step, making them very good at agility contests.

SCOTTISH DEERHOUND

A friendly beast of a dog, a male **SCOTTISH DEERHOUND** might weigh more than one hundred pounds and stand almost three feet tall. Along with a very long neck, it boasts one of the most unusual coats in color and texture: a dark gray that's almost blue and grows in crunchy and hard. Nicknamed "the Royal Dog of Scotland," it was present in the country before Scotland was established in the tenth century. They were once wild dogs that clan chieftains utilized to track and hunt the wild red deer.

SCOTTISH TERRIER

Known as "the Diehard," this little dog is full of independence and energy. Its bright eyes and sharply pointed ears indicate a natural readiness—Scotties were bred to be watchdogs and small-animal hunters in the rocky Scottish Highlands. In the seventeenth century, England's Scotland-born King James I loved **SCOTTISH TERRIERS** so much that he gave them as gifts. In the 1930s and 1940s, they were the small dog of choice for movie stars and politicians—President Franklin D. Roosevelt was rarely seen without his Scottie, Fala.

SHETLAND SHEEPDOG

Better known as the sheltie, this herding dog comes from the rugged Shetland Islands off Scotland. **SHETLAND SHEEPDOGS** look and act like collies—they're just smaller and more active because they were bred down from those dogs. On the remote and very cold Shetland Islands, food can be scarce, and its residents needed a sheepherding farm dog that required as little food as possible. The sheltie was virtually unknown to the outside world, even the rest of the United Kingdom, until the early 1900s.

SHIBA INU

The **SHIBA INU** could be found in the mountains of Japan as far back as 300 BC. *Shiba Inu* translates to "brushwood dog," referring to the brush around the mountains that the dogs originally lived in. During World War II, the Shiba Inu almost went extinct, but its popularity spread when an American military family stationed in Japan brought one back to the United States in 1954. In the twenty-first century, this breed is very popular across the internet. The doge meme started when a funny photo of a Shiba named Kabosu went viral.

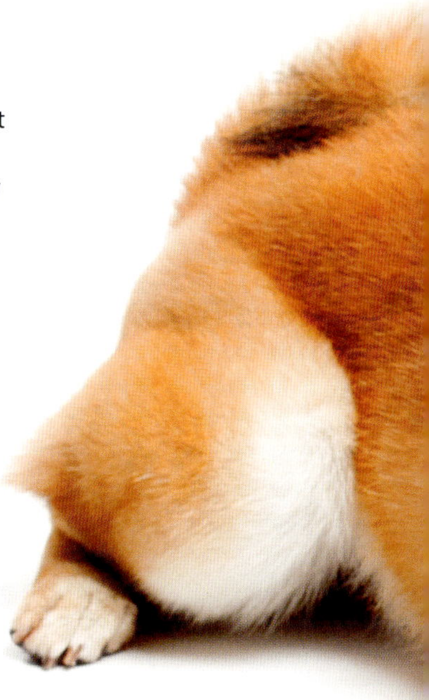

SHIH TZU

This delicate, silky-haired, tiny dog is more closely related to a wolf than any other tiny dog breed. The **SHIH TZU** was first bred two thousand years ago. It was created by crossing a Lhasa apso and Pekingese to be companions to members of the Chinese imperial court. Their main job was to lie on their master's feet at night to keep them warm in the cold weather. Following the Chinese revolution in 1949, the shih tzu nearly went extinct with only fourteen left. However, the breed made an incredible comeback and is now one of the top ten most popular dog breeds in the United States. All shih tzus alive today are related to those fourteen dogs from China.

SIBERIAN HUSKY

Nome, Alaska, suffered a diphtheria epidemic in 1925, and a blizzard prevented medical professionals from reaching the town. A team of **SIBERIAN HUSKIES**, with their furry toes, thick coats, and catchy claws, carried a sled into Nome with the serum that was used to save hundreds of lives. Brought from the Siberia region of northeastern Russia all the way to Alaska in the early 1900s, Siberian huskies can withstand -50°F temperatures and run for hours because of their thick coats of fur, which protect them from the cold.

SILKY TERRIER

Originating from Sydney, this dog is the Australian cousin of the similarly small and equally energetic breed from England called the Yorkshire terrier. English settlers brought Yorkshire terriers with them to Australia in the 1700s, and the **SILKY TERRIER** descended from those dogs. However, the silky terrier has its own unique qualities. Their oval-shaped eyes and shiny, fine hair, which falls on the dog's triangular head and naturally parts in the middle, make them look a bit more like people than do most dogs.

SOFT-COATED WHEATEN TERRIER

This adorable terrier is known for the wave of fur that grows down its curly face. The **SOFT-COATED WHEATEN TERRIER** is one of the few dogs that doesn't shed. However, these dogs need to be brushed or else their curls can get knotted easily. A popular dog for farmers in Ireland in the 1700s, this breed offered a lot of help and would get pampered in return. They're so friendly and loyal that farmers broke tradition and brought these dogs inside at night, treating them like pets. Before that, most dogs had to sleep outside in the cold!

STANDARD SCHNAUZER

There are three breeds of schnauzer—miniature, standard, and giant—but the **STANDARD SCHNAUZER**, which emerged in the Bavaria region of Germany in the Middle Ages, is the original stock. Until the nineteenth century, these canines were strictly working and utility dogs, but nobles soon took notice and decided they wanted to keep schnauzers as pets. The miniature and giant breeds look a lot like the original standard, with a hairy, whisker-laden face and snout, and ears that curiously point up and out.

WEIMARANER

Made famous by the popular funny photographs that William Wegman began taking of his dogs in the 1970s, the **WEIMARANER** is a tall, elegant, and graceful dog. It has a one-of-a-kind silver-gray coat and blue-gray or amber eyes. Because of these special features, the Weimaraner was given the nickname "the Grey Ghost." Bred in Germany to hunt deer and boar, this dog made its way to the United States in the early 1900s. The Weimaraner is known for its extremely sensitive nose—it can sniff out most anything.

WELSH TERRIER

The **WELSH TERRIER** looks like a miniature version of the giant Airedale. This is because the two breeds have a common ancient ancestor, the Old English Black and Tan. The calmest of all the hole-digging terriers, this breed was created in the 1700s to be fox-hunting dogs in the northern mountains of Wales. Owners realized that the Welsh terrier's strong paws and mighty jaw also made it skilled at getting rid of pests like otters and badgers.

WHIPPET

When the **WHIPPET** was developed in England in the late 1800s, the new breed was so speedy that their name is believed to come from "whip it," English slang meaning "to move quickly." Most of this dog's features were designed for its original purpose: rabbit hunting. Their long necks allow them to see far distances, and their powerful eyes can see well even in the dark. Whippets can run as fast as thirty-five miles per hour. They can get all four paws off the ground twice in one movement, making a running whippet look like it is flying.

WIRE FOX TERRIER

Popular in the United States in the 1930s, 1940s, and 1950s, the **WIRE FOX TERRIER** starred in movies like *The Thin Man* and *Bringing Up Baby*. This adorable dog boasts a uniquely rectangular nose and a wiry beard. Its tail is often set high and straight, moving based on the dog's mood and energy level. This strong tail is functional, too. Owners were able to grab wire fox terriers safely by their tails if they got stuck while tracking small animals. Feisty and energetic, wire fox terriers bark and bounce when they're excited.

WIREHAIRED POINTING GRIFFON

In the Netherlands, hunters needed a dog that could be strong and swift on land and also swim well. This is why they created the **WIREHAIRED POINTING GRIFFON**, a web-toed dog that could retrieve ducks from waterways. These dogs have low-shedding coats. Their fur is gritty to the touch and not at all soft, which is all the better to protect them while they are in water. Long, lanky, and tall, this breed makes an excellent family dog because it is loyal and easily trained.

YORKSHIRE TERRIER

Affectionately known as Yorkies, these dogs weigh between five and seven pounds and stand from seven to eight inches tall. **YORKSHIRE TERRIERS** were bred to catch rats in nineteenth-century English factories. Shortly after, they became a chosen dog among high society, because they're happy to sit around lazily. They are known for letting their owners style their hair in creative ways with bows and clips. They have hair similar to human hair—it lacks the fine particles called dander, which is what people allergic to dogs can't tolerate. For this reason, Yorkies are popular with those who are allergic to dogs but still want a canine companion.

RESOURCES

Built on the long legacy of TIME, TIME for Kids has been a trusted news source in schools for more than 30 years, providing educators with valuable resources for the classroom. From articles about new scientific breakthroughs to profiles on inspiring kids who are helping their communities, TIME for Kids has content to inspire every reader.

Learn more about dogs and other interesting animals with TIME for Kids!

Visit **www.timeforkids.com** and explore the **Animals** topic to discover your next favorite species.

ADOPT A DOG TODAY!

In 2024 alone, 5.8 million homeless cats and dogs entered animal shelters. On a more positive note, 4.2 million shelter animals were adopted in 2024. Of those 4.2 million adoptees, 2 million of them were dogs. If your family is planning to add a furry friend to your household, consider adopting a rescue dog from one of the following websites:

American Society for the Prevention of Cruelty to Animals: www.aspca.org

Petfinder: www.petfinder.com

Adopt a Pet: www.adoptapet.com

TRAINING TIPS!

If you already have a puppy or dog within your home, you can train it to do a variety of different things! Training a dog can be as simple as teaching it to sit on command or as advanced as teaching it to run an agility course. Whatever it is you're hoping to teach your canine to do, you can find tips on how to get started through the expertise of the American Kennel Club. Find articles full of tips and tricks at the website below!

AKC Training Tips: www.akc.org/expert-advice/training